Family

cowboy boot

Grandma Thora

toy bunny

alarm clock

lollipop

braces

handkerchief

footstool

Grandpa Dave

toothpaste

doll's pram

pudding

baby bottle

rubber duck

toothbrush

D.W.

Baby Kate

dummy

For
Janet Schulman, F.C.E.
(first class editor)

A Red Fox Book
Published by Random House Children's Books
20 Vauxhall Bridge Road, London SW1V 2SA
A division of Random House UK Ltd
London Melbourne Sydney Auckland
Johannesburg and agencies throughout the world

Copyright © 1997 by Marc Brown

First published in the USA by Random House Inc., New York
and simultaneously in Canada by
Random House of Canada Limited, Toronto
First published in Great Britain by Red Fox 1998
3 5 7 9 10 8 6 4
Printed in Singapore
Random House UK Limited Reg. No. 954009
ISBN 0 09 926392 0

scissors

hairbrush

lizard

pen

T-shirt

belt

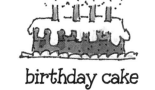
birthday cake

slippers

pyjamas

spaghetti

drum

vest

ARTHUR'S REALLY HELPFUL WORD BOOK

MARC BROWN

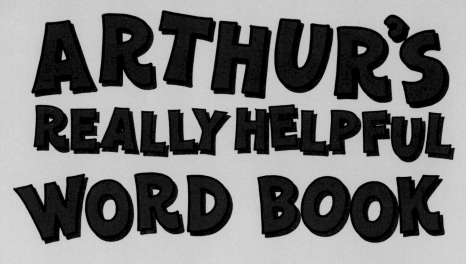

balloon

RED FOX

party hat

baby powder

telephone

anchor

recorder

beads
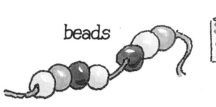

present

fireplace

roof

shutters

highchair

towel

soap dish

shower curtain

mirror

paintbrush

shampoo

door

tap

toilet

washbasin

bath

At Arthur's House

Saturday is clean-up day and everyone is busy. What are some of the things you can do to help around your house?

staircase

piano

chair

telephone

awning

chest

table

light switch

fuse box

stairs

tools

oilcan

dirty clothes

vice

work-bench

light bulb

hot water tank

tins of paint

matches

iron

needle and thread

ironing board

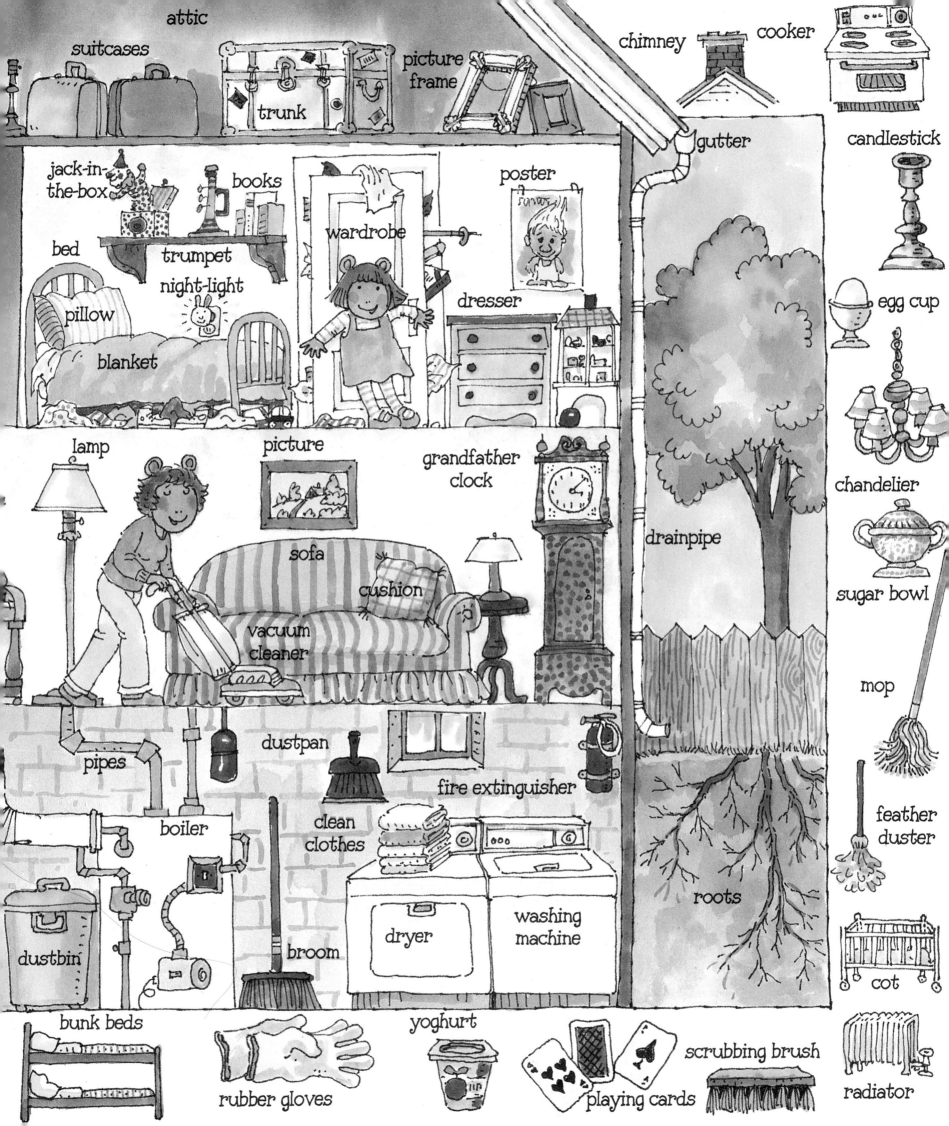

attic

suitcases

trunk

picture frame

chimney

cooker

gutter

candlestick

jack-in-the-box

books

poster

egg cup

bed

trumpet

wardrobe

night-light

dresser

pillow

blanket

chandelier

lamp

picture

grandfather clock

drainpipe

sugar bowl

sofa

cushion

vacuum cleaner

mop

pipes

dustpan

feather duster

boiler

clean clothes

fire extinguisher

dustbin

broom

dryer

washing machine

roots

cot

bunk beds

yoghurt

scrubbing brush

rubber gloves

playing cards

radiator

shark

crocodile

deer

elephant

lion

At the Zoo

Watching the sea lions is always fun but today there is some real monkey business going on at the zoo. All of the monkeys have escaped. Can you help the zoo keeper find them?

zebra

giraffe

ticket booth

bird

ostrich

turnstile

zoo keeper

pushchair

panda

camel

dolphin

tiger

penguin

buffalo

leopard

hippopotamus

snake

parrots

hoop

fish

bucket

horse

ball

sea lion

turtle

balloons

gorilla

ICE CREAM

dog

anteater

polar bear

fox

peacock

A armadillo
B beehive
C clown
D dolphin
E ear

Z zip
Y yarn
X x-ray
W whale
V violin
U unicorn
T tea kettle
S skateboard

At School with D.W.

Everyone is very busy at school today, including the class gerbil.
He likes stories too!

bobble hat
lunch box
plant
cactus
calendar
blackboard
MAY
ELIZA TOJON
toy refrigerator
coat rack
mittens
cage
boots
glove puppet
top hat
toy cooker
saucepan
toy sink
easel
high heels
crown
cowboy hat
paintbrush

Counting

From 1 to 10 – can you count these city things?

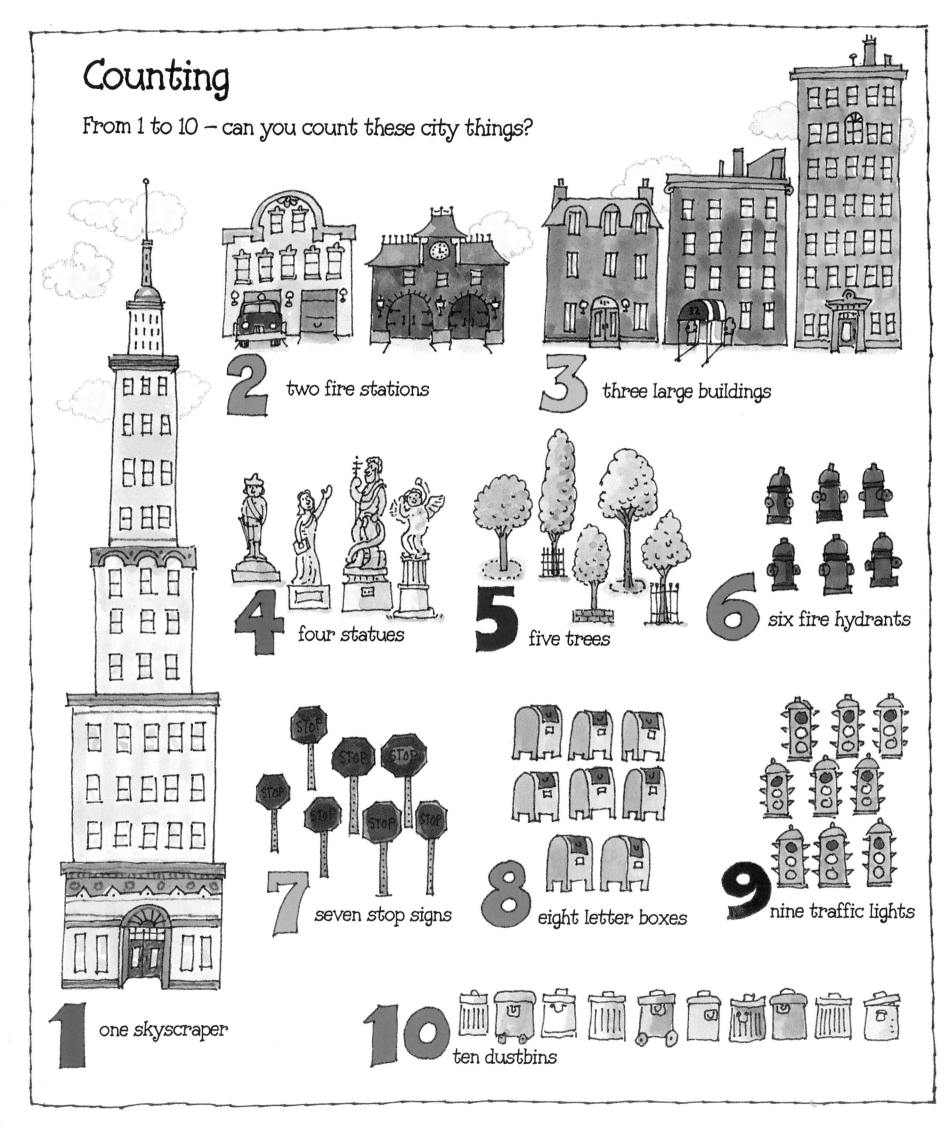

2 two fire stations

3 three large buildings

4 four statues

5 five trees

6 six fire hydrants

7 seven stop signs

8 eight letter boxes

9 nine traffic lights

1 one skyscraper

10 ten dustbins

Opposites

Do you know any others? Yes? No?

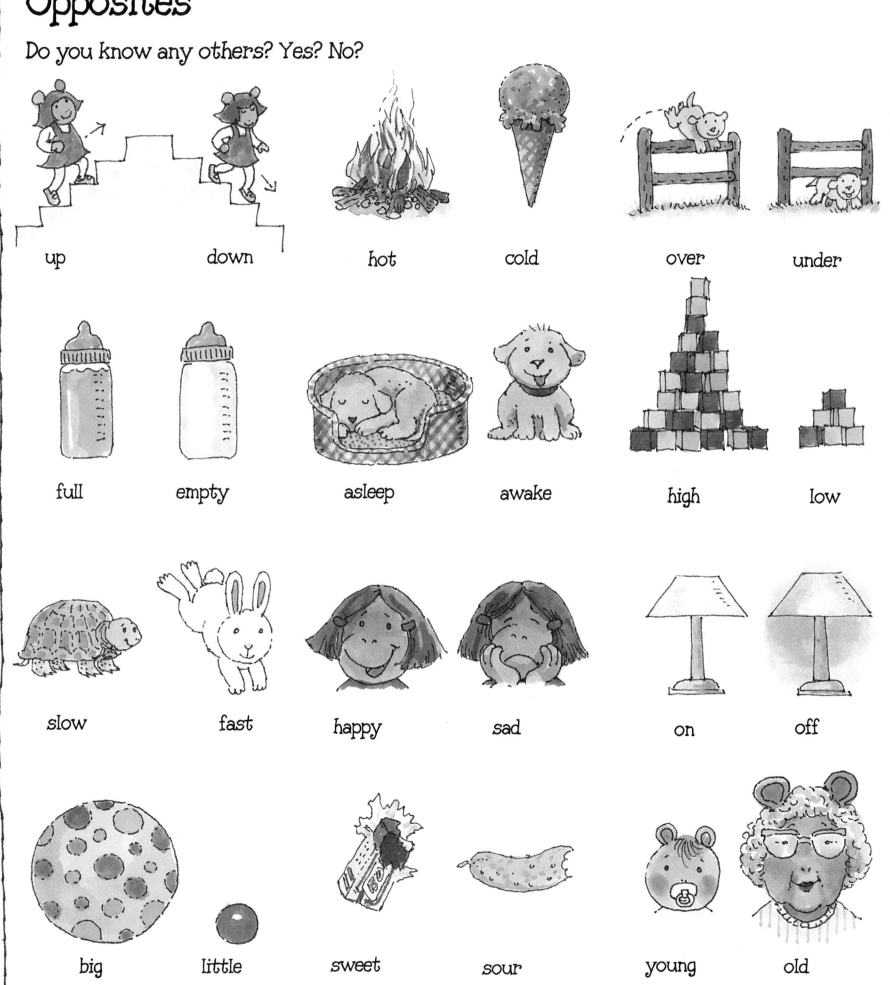

up   down   hot   cold   over   under

full   empty   asleep   awake   high   low

slow   fast   happy   sad   on   off

big   little   sweet   sour   young   old

The Big
Bad Wolf

Jack
and the
beanstalk

giant

castle

sword

princess

dragon

knight in armour

The Three
Little Pigs

Little
Red
Riding
Hood

Grandma

GREAT STORIES

Storyland

Arthur loves to read stories.

He also likes to make up his own.

Would you like to make up a *story*?

Goldilocks

The Three Bears

Cinderella

prince

planet

spacesuit

antennae

alien

spaceship

gingerbread house

Hansel and Gretel

witch

flag

sails

Humpty Dumpty

ship

pirate

cannons

treasure chest

Tinker Bell

Peter Pan

At the Supermarket

Arthur has to do some shopping. Can you help him find everything on his list?

peaches

ice cream

banana

raspberries

ketchup

pear

lime

aubergine

peas

lettuce

toilet paper

MEAT

chicken

butcher

steaks

sausages

HOUSEHOLD

paper towels

BAKERY

rolls

bread

cakes

cereal
pineapple
eggs
paper towels
bread

shopping trolley

apples

soap

flour

jam

celery

cucumber

tissues

batteries

lemon

cantaloupe

washing-up liquid

tuna fish

kiwi fruit

garlic

beetroot

mustard

orange

juice

SPECIAL

pineapples

CEREAL

bagels

DAIRY

muffins

yoghurt

butter

soup

cheese

pie

milk

eggs

Swiss cheese

spaghetti

pepper

sauce

watermelon

juice

gloves

snowball

cap

hockey stick

hockey puck

valentine

thermometer

snowflakes

fire hydrant

icicles

snow shovel

bird feeder

scarf

pipe

snowman

snowsuit

boots

Winter

It's a snowy day, and the
whole world is covered in white.
But there are some bright red things that stand out.
How many can you find?

mitten

bird

skis

poles

ice skates

goggles

earmuffs

toboggan

birdbath

gate

toad

letter box

tricycle

roller skates

eggs

nest

triangle

square

chimney

circle

diamond

roof

bone

butterfly

string

fence

rainhat

raincoat

helmet

wellington boots

stabilizers

umbrella

bicycle

tulip

crocus

robin

daffodil

Spring

It is a beautiful day for flying kites and
having fun! These kites are all different shapes.
What shapes can you see?

puddle

snail

rake

hose

trowel

seeds

flowerpot

watering can

 fan

 ice cream van

ice cream cone

ice lolly

 lobster

 sunblock... sandals

Summer

A picnic at the beach is delicious on a hot summer's day. The ants think so too. How many ants came to Arthur's picnic?

lighthouse

cliff

sailing boat

motorboat

buoy

wave

sand dune

beach ball

beach bag

swimming costume

picnic basket

crisps

cup

plate

beach blanket

shell

sandwich

spade

bucket

sand castle

seagull

ants

starfish

 lawnmower

 sunglasses

 beach umbrella

 crab

 jug

 dandelion

seeds

skeletons
turkey
moth
squirrel
acorn
wheelbarrow

branches
knife
window
leaves
tree
bush
happy
jack-o'-lanterns
sad
surprised
pumpkin
jumper
rake

Autumn

D.W. is helping Arthur rake the leaves.
Father is getting ready for Hallowe'en.
What kinds of faces has he carved?

American football
gourds
witch
bat
ghost
wheat
mask

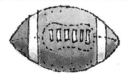

bull

cherries

calf

goose

tomato

wheatsheaves

hoe

milk can

At Grandpa Dave's Farm

Arthur is learning how to milk a cow. The cow has something to say about that: Moooooooo! What do some of the other animals say?

Oink-oink

Mooooooooo

pig

pigsty

cow

cowbell

fly

tail

Meow-meow

udder

pail

cat

stool

mouse horseshoe

hay cart

onions

watch

medicine

jellybeans

weighing scales

shoes

French fries

television

popcorn

sweets

dress

perfume

paints and brushes

BANK

ATM

Ice Cream Shop

escalator

CINEMA

NOW SHOWING

BIONIC BUNNY ON MARS

PRETTY PONY, COME HOME

TICKET BOOTH

OUT

IN

walkie-talkie

security guard

At the Shopping Centre

Arthur and D.W. have agreed on a birthday present for their mother. But they can't agree on which film to see. What film do you think they should see?

biscuit

skirt

blouse

hair dryer

radio

soap

dice

video camera

basket

magazine

armchair

toaster

jeans

diamond ring

Book Shop

Toy Shop

sundae

Jewellery

present

bracelet

necklace rings

puppet

doll's house

greetings card

robot

bathrobe

pay phone

fountain

bath brush

litter bin

shopping bag

tennis racket

shorts

sledge

newspaper

underwear

milkshake

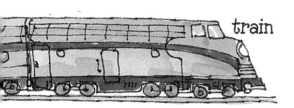
train

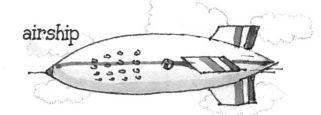
airship

submarine

Things That Go

What's your favourite way to get from here to there?

delivery van

Renita's Flowers

Honk! Honk!

Screech!

bicycle

RELIABLE MOVERS

removal lorry

Honk! Honk!

taxi

Beep! Beep! Beep! Beep!

TAXI

Whee-eeee! Whee-eee!

police car

POLICE

Piccadilly Circus

racing car

bulldozer

jeep

oil tanker

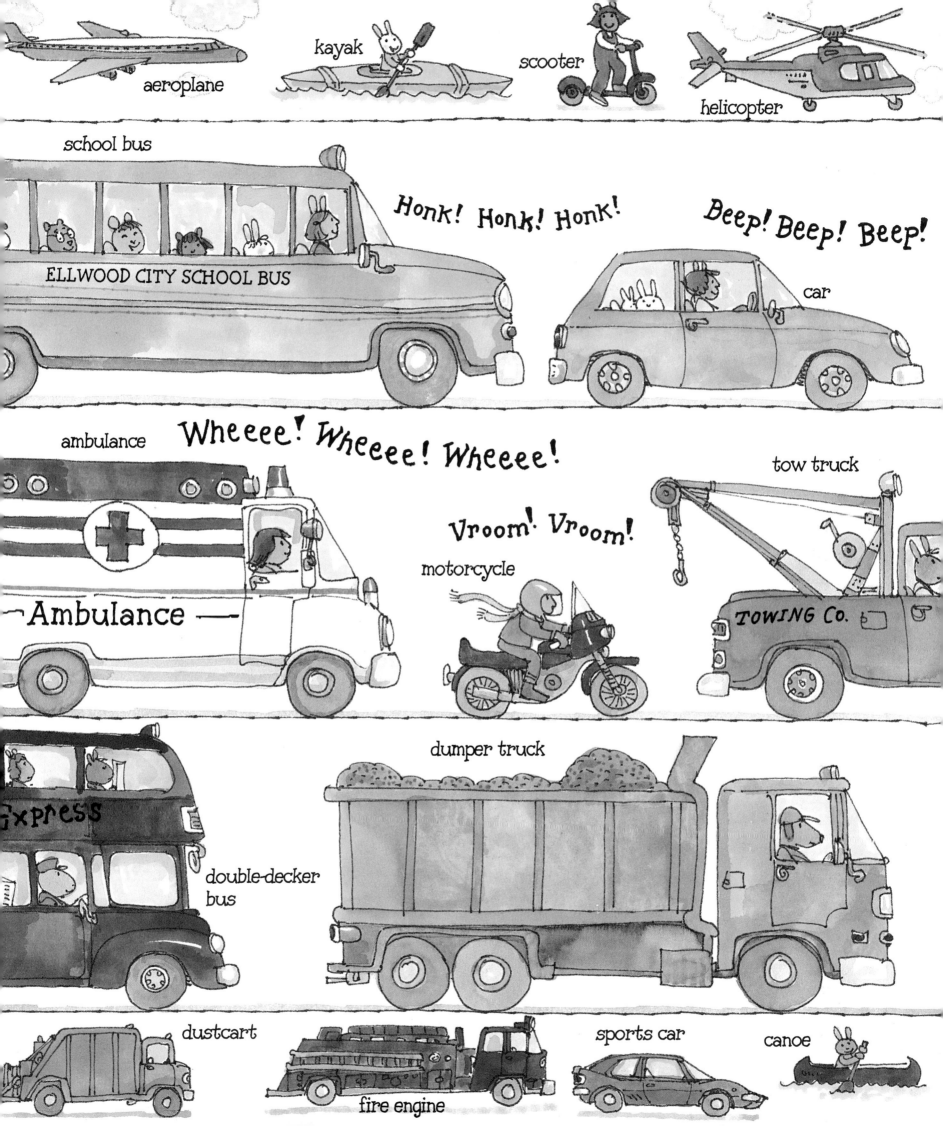

swimming pool

star

lantern

sports bag

compass

cool box

Thermos flask

sleeping bag

first aid kit

insect repellent

firewood

Camping in the Garden

Telling spooky stories around the camp-fire can make you imagine all sorts of strange things. What can you see in the clouds?

clouds

smoke

log

marshmallows

water bottle

fire

torch

raisins

fishing rod

fish

fishing net

ping-pong bat

ping-pong ball

tadpole

hammock

tennis ball

moth

dragonfly

fly

fly swatter

owl

moon

fireflies

sky

fern

birdhouse

tent

snail

hot dog

binoculars

magnifying glass

blanket

pillow

raccoon

mushroom

worm

skunk

What's Inside?

Baby Kate has turned everything upside down. What a mess! Can you help Arthur and D.W. put everything back where it belongs?

COOKIES

MILK

tool box

purse

tissues

pen

keys

lipstick

comb

chewing gum

notebook

building blocks

truck

teddy bear

doll

toy

yo-yo

lunch box

screws

screwdriver

pliers

nails

hammer

drill

tape measure

handbag

cookie

carrot sticks

juice

sandwich

apple

napkin

toy box

When Arthur Grows Up...

Here are some of the things he might be.

astronaut

fireman

policeman

cowboy

soldier

doctor

artist

rock star

teacher

chef

jester

construction worker

calculator

marker pen

ring binder

envelope

stamp

hole punch

Mother at Work

Mother is an accountant. D.W. loves to visit her office. There are so many interesting things there, including a mouse that doesn't eat cheese. Can you find it?

lamp

pictures

pin board

mug

briefcase

TAXES

computer

telephone

desk

drawer

important letters

wastepaper basket

files

stapler

carpet

paperclip

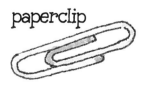

sticky tape

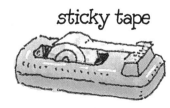

rubber bands

pencil sharpener

drawing pin

eraser

tack

wooden spoon   biscuit cutters   measuring spoons   birthday candles   tongs   salt   pepper   timer

Father at Work

Arthur's father is a caterer. Sometimes Arthur helps him clean up.

He is very good at licking the spoons.

coffee

cooking oil

fridge magnets

cupboard

microwave oven

washing-up liquid

freezer

refrigerator

cake

sink

jam

blender

whisk

mixing bowl

spatula

icing bag

cooking pot

dishwasher

pasta

flour

rice

sugar

frying pan

colander

tray

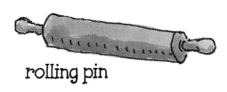

rolling pin

pan holder

sponge

measuring jug

electric mixer

bench

dandelion

stream

bridge

swan

clover

pigeon

spinning top

sweatshirt

rings

climbing frame

litter bin

In the Playground

D.W. is playing hide-and-seek and she is 'it'. Can you help her find Arthur, Muffy, Francine and Binky? (Their pictures are on the last two pages.)

swings

...ready or not, here I come!

sand

sand pit

bucket

grass

seesaw

pussywillow

jacks

spider

plaster

whistle

ladybird

slide

lunch box

skipping rope

lamppost

basketball hoop

bouncing ball

ladder

bell

playhouse

basketball

merry-go-round

squirrel

caterpillar

pogo stick

water lily

hopscotch game

pavement

sun

sand toys

trike

marbles

buttons

bottle tops

stamps

dolls

marbles

pencils

Diplodocus

Cetiosaurus

Collections

Buster has quite a collection of toy dinosaurs! People can collect all sorts of things. Do you have a collection?

caps

rocks

postcards

feathers

toy cars

coins

Stegosaurus

Triceratops

Allosaurus

shells

Tyrannosaurus rex

action figures

trading cards

teddy bears

ballet shoes

Arthur's

star

tooth

moon

Binky Barnes

Prunella

flippers

guitar

crisps

noughts and crosses

plaits

bubble gum

Arthur

tambourine

Buster

Muffy